I0424924

CONTENTS

IN CRISIS

I t was September 26th, 2018, just a few weeks after school had started and I was putting the kids to bed. It was an average day, with me going to work the kids going to school and the after-school sitter meeting my younger two at the bus stop and staying with them until I got home from work. My oldest son (12 years old) went to boy scouts that night and had a great time. My younger two were already tucked in their beds and I was putting my oldest to sleep.

"Mom, we have to get rid of that sitter, I think she's bad."

"Why do you think she's bad?"

"I don't know, she's just bad. You need to fire her."

"I'm not going to fire her for no reason. Everyone loves her and we thought she was the best out of the 3 sitters we interviewed."

"No, you have to get rid of her."

"Stop it! I'm not firing her unless you can give me a good reason. I can't fire someone just because you think she's bad, especially when she hasn't done anything bad."

"MOM... Something is VERY wrong... I need to talk to you."

"You need to go to sleep. It's getting late and you have school tomorrow."

"NO! SOMETHING IS WRONG!! We need to get out of my bedroom

and turn the lights on so that I can talk to you. This is VERY important!"

The rest of that night is somewhat blurry. We were up for hours talking about things that don't really make any sense, answering questions that didn't make any sense either... "I'm worried that you are not really my mom. I think you're an imposter who is just trying to look like my mom. You look different. You don't look like my mom. Look – here is a picture of my mom and you don't look like that right now. Your arms look bigger and more muscular. Your nail polish looks different. When did you get your nails painted? They weren't like that before. Do you have something sharp in your pockets that could hurt me? We need to keep the lights on..."

There were more questions like that All. Night. Long. My ex-husband came over and sat with us for a while providing reassurance that I really was who I said I was – and I was not an imposter. He eventually left, but the questions (and my attempts at reassurance) continued throughout the night. We got a couple of hours of sleep, finally passing out from sheer exhaustion – with the lights still on and my son lying next to me in bed so he could keep an eye on me.

Was this a side-effect of the ADHD medication he had tolerated well for over 3 years? Maybe it wasn't working the same after we had taken a break from it over the summer? I poured through the label of the ADHD meds and saw that psychosis and paranoia were possible side effects. We had never experienced this before, but it was the only explanation I had for why we had just experienced what we had that night.

"You're staying home from school today," I said. "I think you're having side effects from your ADHD medication and I'm going to call your doctor." Our pediatrician wasn't in that day, but I explained to the nurse what had happened, and she said she'd call back after consulting with the other doctors who were there. After about 20 minutes or so, I got a call back from the nurse, who told me this was not from the ADHD meds, because that medication would have been out of the system by evening.

She told me to go to the ER and tell them my child was experiencing a mental health crisis. I almost lost it, but somehow stayed calm and looked through my pill bottles to see if I had any Ativan left. I almost never take this anti-anxiety medicine, and I wasn't sure I even had any left. My doctor prescribed this for me when I was going through my divorce, and I have taken it to calm down during various mini-crises in my life. I took one, then called my ex-husband to let him know that I'd been instructed to go to the ER.

He met us there, and we waited quietly to get checked in. A man with a strange gait kept walking in and out of the doors for the crisis center, mumbling to himself. He looked like he hadn't showered in a long time, and his clothes were so big on him, they were practically falling off. The security guard near the entrance to the crisis center politely asked him to pull up his pants. He eventually left, and they escorted us into what appeared to be a meeting room. We shared our story with someone who was either a therapist or an administrative assistant. She asked a bunch of questions, took a bunch of notes, and then we waited to see a doctor.

The doctor walked in, asked more questions, determined that my son was not at imminent risk of hurting himself or someone else, and then told us to get an appointment with a psychiatrist and a therapist. She also recommended stopping the ADHD medication completely. She gave us the names of two psychiatry practices (one of which she told us was probably no longer accepting new patients due to all the referrals she sent their way) and then released us, telling us to keep a close eye on things and to come right back to the ER if anything similar happened again.

After leaving the ER, I called the other practice on her list, left a voicemail explaining in detail what had just happened, and waited for a call back. After several hours with no return call, I filled out the detailed patient intake form on their practice website, submitted it online and called again, only to leave another message on voicemail.

The next morning, we were going to try to go to school. We were told to stop the ADHD medication for now, and I was worried about how that might impact school. But we went to the bus stop and faced the day. Before we left, my son said he needed to speak to me: "Mom, *please* don't get mad at me for saying this, because I know you're my mom, but could you *please* just promise me that you *really are* my mom and you're not somebody else pretending to be my mom?" My heart sank. At this point, I knew for sure that all his ADHD medication was completely out of his system because it had been well over 24 hours. But I think I was still hanging onto hope that this was just a horrible new side effect of the meds. I would come to find it was way more complicated than that.

About 45 minutes later, I received a call from the school nurse. School was just too difficult for him to face, and now he was panicked that something bad was going to happen to one of his parents during the day. He was certain that one of us was going to get into a bad car accident as we drove to work. So, I called my ex-husband, we picked him up from school and brought him to the ER again, not knowing what else to do.

On the way to the ER, I left a 3rd message on the psychiatry office voicemail, letting them know that we were heading back to the ER and asking them to please call me back to let me know if they could help me. I could no longer wait to get my son help and needed to find another psychiatrist if they weren't able to help. I received a message from their office later that afternoon saying they couldn't help us, because they didn't think they were "a good fit" for my son.

This 2nd ER visit was more of the same. We met with someone who asked us a bunch of questions. They gave us some paperwork to fill out and asked my son for a signature on a contract confirming that he had no desire to hurt himself or others. Then, they gave us a much longer list of psychiatrists to call. They said it would be hard to get an appointment with a psychiatrist any-time in the next few weeks and suggested we consider a partial inpatient program that started on Monday. They said that would be only way to get him in to see a psychiatrist right away, and it would mean driving him to a mental hospital during the day in-stead of school, and then bringing him home at night. This was a frightening option, but something we were considering, espe-cially if he couldn't make it through a school day.

On the way home, I was determined to find help for my son before the weekend. It was a Friday, it was late morning, and I knew I only had a few hours left before offices began to shut down for the week. We stopped at McDonald's to get a snack at the drive-thru before we went home to start making phone calls.

"Mom, my smoothie tastes funny, and I'm getting a headache. Do you think they put something bad in my smoothie?"

"No, honey. You are just very tired from not getting much sleep over the past couple of days. Stress and lack of sleep can cause headaches."

"I think there's poison in my drink. I'm worried. They put some-thing bad in here and it's causing my headache. I can't drink this anymore."

I started making phone calls and leaving lots of messages. Psychi-atrists and therapists are usually in session during the day and they don't always have office staff available to answer the phone. I finally reached a human who answered the phone at a local ther-apy group. I told her what had been going on and asked if I could bring my son in to talk to someone that afternoon. She told me they don't schedule same day appointments, and I asked her to please just check to see if there had been any cancellations. I told her more about what had been happening over the past couple of days and how much I needed to get my son help before going into the weekend. She put me on hold, and miraculously, she found a cancellation and contacted a therapist who agreed to meet with us that afternoon.

I continued making calls until I found a psychiatry office that had a cancellation on that upcoming Monday and locked that appointment in before heading to the therapist. I was feeling a little better, knowing that we were going to see someone who could give us some strategies to get through the weekend – and hopefully some answers to why this was happening.

The therapist was a young, friendly woman and she connected with us right away. She gave my son some breathing strategies to use and I could sense the tension starting to drift away from him a little bit. We made a follow up appointment with her for the next week and went home, still unsure of what would come next.

That Monday, we went to the psychiatry office and met with a therapist for the intake process. After meeting with her, she explained how their treatment program worked. We would have to meet with that practice's therapist – and commit to ongoing weekly therapy with her - in order to get an appointment with the psychiatrist at that office. We could've made that work and continue to see the first therapist who we liked, but as we walked out of the office and back to the car, I realized this wouldn't be possible.

"I don't like that lady. She's a little strange."

"What don't you like about her?" I asked.

"I don't know, I just have a bad feeling about her."

I pulled the list of psychiatrists out of my folder the next morning and began making calls and leaving voicemails. I called our pediatrician's office again and asked for a call back so that I could discuss the ADHD meds and give the pediatrician an update on what was happening.

I spent hours calling people, asking if someone, *anyone,* could see my son. Many were not accepting new patients or couldn't get us in for 3-4 weeks – and I still had a child who wasn't sure if I was really who I said I was. My son was asking me to show him that my fingerprint worked to unlock my phone, he grilled me constantly to see if I remembered childhood experiences and family vacations, and he was always looking at me at in a questioning, "*stranger danger*" kind of way.

Later that day, a psychiatrist called me back and agreed to meet with me in about a week, and then meet with my son a few days later, if we decided to proceed with an evaluation. That wasn't fast enough for me, but at least I had booked an appointment. My son was going back to school, but he could no longer walk to the bus alone. He needed me to stay with him until the bus picked him up, and then he needed to call one more time as soon as he got to school and before he had to put his phone in his locker for the day. We notified the school's guidance counselor, the school psychologist and his teachers about what was going on, and the school issued him a "gold pass" that allows him to leave the classroom to visit the nurse or guidance at any time. This was helpful, because he frequently had to visit the nurse to call one of us to make sure we were OK. He was still worried that one of us would get hurt in a car accident.

The following day -- a full week following the onset of psychosis, or paranoia, or anxiety, or *whatever* was going on, I sat down to make some more phone calls. I called the pediatrician's office again and begged the nurse to have the doctor call me back. My son wasn't taking ADHD meds, he was back to school and he was really struggling. He called me back rather quickly and confirmed that the ADHD meds did not cause these symptoms and agreed that we should no longer give him the meds considering what was going on.

I asked if there was anything he could do to help us because I was having trouble getting a psychiatry appointment. He told me that we had made tremendous progress by attending therapy and even getting a psychiatry appointment in less than 3 weeks. He said it was "normal" to have to wait 3-4 weeks for treatment and he was surprised that we were able to get these appointments so quickly.

I got off the phone with the doctor, shut the door to my office and burst into tears. My mind raced.

The progress I was making was GOOD? It's normal for a child experiencing psychosis to have to wait 3-4 weeks to see a mental health professional - assuming they aren't at risk of harming themselves or others? The only way for me to get help from a psychiatrist was to bring my son to a Mental Hospital during the day for partial inpatient treatment?

How can this be "normal?" My kid thinks I am a stranger pretending to be his Mom! I'm being asked if I am putting poison on his toast at breakfast time, and there is no medical doctor who can see my child unless I commit him to an in-patient hospital? What if I'm stabbed in the middle of the night because I am thought to be an "imposter" and someone who may be dangerous? Why am I being told <u>this is just the way it is</u>?

I missed my next meeting as I cried silently in my office for a half hour, just letting everything out. Then, I pulled myself together and made more phone calls. I can't even count the number of phone calls I made, but I called every single phone number I could find for a child psychiatrist within about an hour drive of where we live.

Miraculously, somebody finally answered the phone and told me that one of the partners had an opening the following morning at 9:00 am. Of course, they didn't accept my insurance, but I didn't care – My son was going to finally speak to a medical doctor and we were going to figure out how to make these intrusive thoughts go away.

I also started doing research on mental health care for children and was horrified by the information I found:

- A child experiencing a mental health crisis (including one who is experiencing psychosis) should expect to wait 3-4 weeks before seeing a psychiatrist, unless they are at immediate risk of harming themself or others.
- More than 17 million U.S. children are affected by mental health issues annually, according to the Child Mind

Institute.

- There are only 7 thousand mental health professionals in the US who treat children. (This includes all child psychiatrists in full-time practice — along with developmental pediatricians and child psychologists.)
- Treatment within 1-3 years of a patient's first psychotic episode is considered "early intervention."
- Almost half of private psychiatrists do not accept insurance. Of those who do accept insurance, it's difficult to find an in-network psychiatrist (even though the insurance company often has a large list of dead providers,) or those psychiatrists aren't taking new patients, or they see patients for brief med checks but not for psychotherapy.

GETTING A DIAGNOSIS

Our first psychiatry appointment with Dr. T in PA was relatively uneventful. Before the appointment, I typed up a brief medical history, as well as a summary of the events that took place that week and gave it to the doctor because I didn't want to forget to mention something during the appointment. The doctor ordered an MRI and some blood work to rule out anything medical and we scheduled a follow up appointment for the following week to discuss the results of the MRI and bloodwork and talk about next steps for treatment.

The psychiatrist mentioned that he wanted to check the levels of strep antibodies in my son's blood, because strep can sometimes trigger a condition known as PANDAS. He wanted to rule that out before determining a treatment plan. I had heard of PANDAS (Pediatric Autoimmune Neuropsychiatric Disorders Associated with Streptococcal infections) before, because one of my Facebook friends has a son who is dealing with this. Her son's symptoms didn't match what we were dealing with though, so I dismissed it.

I kept the appointment with the other psychiatrist who wanted to meet with just me before meeting my son and met with him later that week. It was another $375 out of pocket and not reimbursed by insurance, but I was taking this very seriously. I explained what was going on, and he said he agreed with the approach the psychiatrist we met with had decided to take. He said he would not have thought to test for PANDAS but would have probably added a tox screen to check for drugs, in case my son took something or was slipped something he wasn't aware about.

I didn't think this could have anything to do with drugs, because my son is very anti-drugs and alcohol. He even worries that I'm killing my brain cells if I have a glass or two of wine. But, I wasn't ruling anything out at this point. Given that he agreed with the other psychiatrist's approach, and it didn't make sense to see 2 psychiatrists at once, we agreed that I would follow up with him if for some reason things didn't work out with the other psychiatrist.

A week later, we had completed our MRI and blood work and were back at the psychiatrist's office to discuss the results. The MRI was thankfully normal. I had prepared myself over the week for a possible brain tumor causing this sudden change in mental state and was glad that wasn't the case. The doctors didn't think it was schizophrenia because he wasn't hearing voices or seeing things, so I really didn't know what was causing this. My son was still questioning me incessantly to confirm that I really was who I said I was, and although he had been going to a behavioral therapist on a weekly basis, I knew his thoughts were not going away.

Dr. T in PA told us that bloodwork was normal, except for an extremely high level of strep antibodies, indicating that PANDAS may be the cause of what we've been experiencing. He told us about a talk he heard from a psychiatrist in Delaware about using IVIG and plasmapheresis to treat PANDAS but said we would have to follow up with our pediatrician to discuss next steps for treatment for that. In the meantime, he said he could help treat the anxiety with an SSRI. We would start at the lowest dose and then go up if needed. We took that prescription and went home.

Over the weekend, my son had tremendous difficulty taking his new meds, because he thought they were bad for him and going to kill him. So, I scheduled another appointment with Dr. T in PA for early that week, and he explained how the meds worked, why he was taking them, and how they could help his worries. After hearing the details from the psychiatrist, my son finally agreed to start taking the meds.

We also brought my son for a strep test to see if the antibodies were related to a current strep virus, and an ear infection check, because his ears had been bothering him. The strep test was negative and his ears were clear - and I began researching PANDAS (Pediatric Autoimmune Neuropsychiatric Disorder Associated with Strep.) I learned that this condition is a subset of PANS (Pediatric Acute-onset Neuropsychiatric Syndrome) which is also an autoimmune condition but is caused by an infection other than strep. It typically presents when a child has a sudden, acute onset of OCD and/or Food Restrictions & multiple neuropsychiatric symptoms, and it's basically a condition where a child's autoimmune system goes haywire and disrupts the neurotransmitters in the brain. I had always thought OCD was when people feel like they have to do things a certain number of times, check things multiple times, arrange things in a specific order, or do things a specific way. All of this is true, but I came to learn that OCD can be so much more than that.

I learned that **Obsessive-Compulsive** Disorder (**OCD**) is a common, chronic and long-lasting disorder in which a person has uncontrollable, reoccurring thoughts (obsessions) and behaviors (compulsions) that repeat over and over. My son was having reoccurring, intrusive thoughts (obsessions) about me being an impostor, people poisoning his food, his parents getting in a car accident, something bad happening to his brother or sister, and the list goes on. He wasn't putting things in a specific order, but this was still OCD due to the obsessive/compulsive nature of his intrusive thoughts.

I also learned that many doctors do not "believe in" PANS/PANDAS because it has only recently been discussed in the medical community, and there haven't been enough studies to validate the condition or its treatment protocol. I read that CHOP (the children's hospital affiliated with our pediatric practice) does not recognize or treat PANS/PANDAS, but still made an appointment with our pediatrician. Knowing that CHOP pediatricians are typically "by the book" when it comes to following the organization's protocol, I started planning for our pediatrician to turn us away and refer us back to the psychiatrist. So, I began searching for a PANS/PANDAS specialist in our area.

I started our search for a specialist by contacting Dr. E's office at a children's hospital in Delaware. She was the doctor who had given the talk about PANDAS, and the reason why Dr. T in PA had even heard of the condition. Unfortunately, Dr. E was completely booked and was not accepting any new patients. So, I searched a bit more and found Dr. T in NJ, who is a world-renowned PANS/PANDAS specialist.

Dr. T has dedicated his practice to treating children with PANS/PANDAS, and parents fly in from around the country (and even outside of the US) to see him. I called the office to see if I could make an appointment, and the person who answered the phone explained that they do not take insurance, our first appointment would cost $1,000 (with a $250 deposit at the time the appointment is made) and each additional appointment would be $500 throughout treatment.

That was a hard cost to swallow, but of course I agreed to move forward, and I was able to book an appointment for a few weeks later. I knew that my son needed help, and I was willing to do whatever it took for him to get better, even if that meant going bankrupt from medical bills.

It was time for our appointment with the pediatrician, and my son had been complaining of hearing problems over the past week. I really didn't know if the hearing problems were psychosomatic or if he was actually having problems with his ears, so I booked an appointment with a CHOP ENT. When we went for the visit with our pediatrician, my son immediately brought up his hearing problems, so the doctor checked his ears and said he may have some fluid in his ears, but that would go away in time. He thought we should keep the appointment with the ENT to rule out anything else.

I had printed out some information about PANS/PANDAS treatment guidelines from the Journal of Child and Adolescent Psychopharmacology and told our pediatrician that our psychiatrist suspected PANDAS and wanted us to follow up with him. As I suspected, there was no treatment protocol for this at CHOP because there wasn't enough data to support the condition or how to treat it.

Our pediatrician did look it up on his computer though, and he agreed to prescribe a 10-day dose of Amoxicillin because I had showed him some information that indicated that antibiotics have been shown to improve symptoms in PANDAS patients. He warned me about going to see a PANS/PANDAS specialist, saying that they are really expensive, and he was worried about parents getting financially taken advantage of due to the horrific symptoms of this condition and the lack of providers who treat it.

I left the pediatrician that day feeling optimistic that our 10-day course of antibiotics would "cure" my son. I had read about PANS/PANDAS patients who were sick for years, and then got better after just a few days of antibiotics, and I so desperately wanted to have the same experience. However, we saw absolutely no change in my son's condition throughout the 10-days on antibiotics – and to make matters worse, my son saw a sign about the flu shot in the doctor's office and was now convinced he was going to die of the flu. From what I read, the flu shot is not recommended for patients with PANS/PANDAS because their immune system is not working properly and introducing the flu vaccine (or other vaccines) can cause a "flare," making their symptoms even worse. But now my son had "dying from the flu" on his list of intrusive thoughts.

It was still 2 weeks until our appointment with Dr. T in NJ (The PANS/PANDAS specialist, not to be confused with Dr. T in PA, who is our psychiatrist who discovered the high strep antibodies.) I spent every spare minute of my time researching PANS/PANDAS and reading books about it, and my son continued to go to behavioral therapy once a week.

The therapist did not accept my insurance either, but she was amazing and helped my son so much over those weeks prior to treatment. She gave him strategies for how to manage his intrusive thoughts, question their reality and move forward. I truly don't think my son would have been able to manage going to school every day without her help.

At this point, we were stabilized, and my son was managing his symptoms. But the symptoms were still there. My son was still questioning me about poisoning his food, and he still quizzed me occasionally to confirm that I was really his mom. I often wondered if my son was getting better at managing his symptoms or if I was just getting used to the insanity of it all, and to this day, I'm still not certain.

THE PANS/PANDAS SPECIALIST

I t was finally time for our appointment with Dr. T in NJ, and I took the day off work to make the 2-hour drive there for our 2-hour appointment. My ex-husband rode with us in my minivan, and that was a strange experience, because it had been over 6 years since we had taken a car ride together. But, when your son has a psychotic break, you do what you need to do – and the trials and tribulations of the pain caused by divorce seem like merely a blip on your radar.

I was so anxious for this appointment, mainly because I knew Dr. T was an esteemed pediatric neurologist, and one of a very small handful of specialists who treated this condition. I just wanted him to give us a magic pill to make this horrible nightmare go away immediately. But I soon realized that treating this condition was more like a marathon and not at all like a sprint.

Dr. T was a very smart man, and although he was running behind that day and we had to wait over an hour in his waiting room to see him, the appointment was worth the wait. He asked us a bunch of questions and explained PANS/PANDAS to us in simple terms while drawing a diagram of what was happening in my son's body to cause these neuropsychiatric symptoms.

He told us that he wanted to test for other antibodies that could be contributing to my son's condition, because although his strep titers (antibodies) were higher-than-normal, there could be other infections that were even further outside of the "normal" reference range. Fortunately, Dr. T had a lab right there in his office and we were able to get the blood work done that afternoon. They took 8 vials of blood from my son that day, and it would be another 3 weeks of waiting for test results.

We continued going to behavioral therapy every week and we met with the psychiatrist a couple of times to monitor my son's progress on the SSRI. Dr. T from PA (the psychiatrist) thought we needed to increase the dose of the SSRI in order to see improvement and said he would typically have increased the dose by now. However, he didn't want to disrupt anything Dr. T from NJ was planning to do to treat the PANS/PANDAS. So, we remained at the lowest starting dose while we waited to see Dr. T in NJ again.

During this waiting period, my son was going to school every day without taking his ADHD medication and was really struggling in school. We were getting emails from the teachers about how disruptive he was being in the classroom and they were getting very frustrated, even though the school guidance counselor had shared a little bit with them about what was going on and they knew that my son was not able to take his ADHD medicine due to his condition. It got to the point where we had to go to the school for a meeting with the teachers and guidance counselor about my son's 504 plan. The 504 plan was in place previously for his ADHD, but needed to be modified for additional support now that he couldn't take his medication.

On the morning of the meeting with my son's teachers, he asked me before getting on the bus to please reassure him that I was really his mom and not an imposter. So, going into that meeting, I was on edge. I waited in the lobby with my ex-husband and we were brought back to the guidance office, where we waited while a panel of teachers assembled in the conference room.

The day before the meeting, I compiled some flyers from the New

England PANS PANDAS Association which had a brief overview of the condition, along with some common school accommodations for each of the potential symptoms experienced by kids with this condition. I emailed it to the guidance counselor, asking him to forward it to the teachers, and I brought printed copies with me to the meeting. I knew this condition was controversial, and I thought having some information from a third party would help to support our conversation with the teachers.

We entered the conference room and sat uncomfortably across from 4 of my son's teachers as we waited for the guidance counselor. The secretary eventually entered the room and told us that we should get started because the guidance counselor was running behind and still in a meeting with another student. I started the conversation by handing out the flyers I had printed and giving them an overview of how my son's condition started and what we were doing about it. I burst into tears while I was talking and one of the teachers started to get tears in her eyes as she listened to our story.

I stepped out of the room for a bit to compose myself while my ex-husband continued the meeting and was able to calm myself down after about 5 minutes. The teachers were all very compassionate during that meeting and they expressed their desire to help in any way possible.

Following that meeting, the notes from the teachers about my son's behavioral problems in class stopped. I suspect they were horrified by what I had described and didn't want to make matters any worse for us by bringing up the fact that my son couldn't control himself in class. A large percentage of kids with PANS/ PANDAS aren't even able to attend school due to sever separation anxiety and other symptoms. So, the fact that my son was even going to school daily – and keeping his grades up – was a huge accomplishment. I reminded myself of this every time I started to get discouraged about the lack of progress we were making in getting rid of my son's intrusive thoughts.

While waiting for our next appointment with Dr. T in NJ to review blood test results and discuss a treatment program, I was getting daily envelopes in the mail from Quest Diagnostic (the lab that was analyzing the blood work.) As results from the battery of tests came in, another version of the report was mailed out to us and to Dr. T in NJ. One by one, most of the tests were coming back showing very high titers outside of the normal reference range, indicating a previous infection. Some of the tests were inconclusive about whether the infection was a previous one, or still in his system. But all of the infections were common ones that most of us have been exposed to in our lifetime. I learned this by researching every one of them: Epstein Barr, Coxsackie, Herpesvirus 6 and Mycoplasma Pneumonia.

Most people's immune systems produce antibodies that return to normal after the infection leaves, but this is not always the case in people with an autoimmune condition. It's my understanding that in the case of PANS/PANDAS patients, the overactive antibodies impact the brain, causing autoimmune encephalitis which in turn causes neuropsychiatric symptoms presenting as psychiatric illness.

I read a book called "Brain on Fire" about a journalist who suffered from autoimmune encephalitis resulting from an infection, and it sent chills up my spine. Although her symptoms weren't exactly similar to my son's symptoms, there were may parts of her story that described exactly what we were living through – especially the story she told about how she thought her father was an imposter pretending to be her father. Her story had a happy ending, and I was praying that ours would too.

It was finally time for our 2nd appointment with Dr. T in NJ and I went into it optimistic that we would walk away with a treatment plan that would immediately "fix" my son's condition. I wear my rose-colored glasses way too often and am frequently disappointed by my expectations. But, it's my survival mechanism, so that's what I did. Dr. T gave us the following treatment plan, based on my son's current infections and ordered some additional blood work, including a test for Lyme disease, which is another infection known to cause PANS.

Morning	• Fluoxetine (SSRI) • Valtrex 500 mg (antiviral) • Biaxin 500 mg (antibiotic) • B-12 Gummy Vitamin (for low B-12 levels in the blood test)
Afternoon	• Metanx (to help process the B-12) • Culturelle Probiotic (to replace the good bacteria killed by the antibiotic)
Evening	• Valtrex 500 mg (antiviral) • Biaxin 500 mg (antibiotic) • B-12 Gummy Vitamin (for low B-12 levels in the blood test) • Flintstones multivitamin (we were already taking this)

We started taking the pills during the week of Thanksgiving and my son had major GI issues with vomiting, diarrhea and stomach pain that caused him to miss 2 days of school. I called and emailed Dr. T and he said we could stop the antibiotics for a day and then start back at half the dose. We did stop taking the pills on Thanksgiving, because my son wanted to enjoy his Thanksgiving meal, and then we started taking them again the next day. My son didn't want to start taking only half the dose because he really wanted to "get better," so we went back on the full 500 mg twice a day and within a few days, his stomach got used to the medicine.

I was finding it difficult to keep so many pills organized, so I ordered a pill organizer from Amazon with morning, afternoon and evening sections for each day of the week. I would fill it up on Sunday night and all my son's pills were there for each time of the day throughout the week. It was so helpful! I was hoping to see a huge difference in my son's symptoms within a few days after starting the antibiotics, but that didn't happen.

After realizing this wasn't going to be an immediate fix, I started hoping for a difference after a few weeks. That didn't happen either, so I called and emailed Dr. T in NJ to see if we should try another antibiotic. His office told us to have the pharmacy fax in a prescription refill request, and Dr. T would decide at that time on how to proceed. The office staff also told me that the doctor usually keeps patients on the same antibiotic until they are 85% better, so it was no surprise when the pharmacy texted me to let me know that our prescription for Biaxin was ready to be picked up.

SELF-CARE

In January, I made a resolution to focus on self-care. I knew that was going to be incredibly important if I was going to be able to continue moving forward with finding answers to my son's treatment. I had been working tirelessly over the past 3 months, trying to figure out how to help my son and I felt like I was treading water in survival mode, but not getting anywhere. I felt sad, hopeless and unsure of whether we were even on the right treatment path.

My ex-husband and I don't communicate well, but we were able to manage the basics necessary to schedule medical appointments, and we were both on the same page with wanting to do whatever we could to help our son get better. I felt incredibly alone though. I was like I was living in a horror movie and couldn't wake up – and even worse, I was doing it all alone.

My family, friends and coworkers knew what was going on, but if someone asked me how he (or I) was doing, I would burst into tears while talking about it 90% of the time. It was so hard to talk about, so I just stopped talking about it. I would go out to dinner with friends who I don't see on a regular basis and just not mention the hell I was going through at home. I've always been an open book, but this was just too difficult and draining to talk about.

When I did talk about what was going on with my son, people didn't know what to say and I could see and feel the horror inside them while they were processing what I was telling them. That would always abruptly knock my rose-colored glasses off, and I'd see in their eyes how hellish things really were.

When something traumatic or difficult happens to us, whether it's episodic or chronic, we naturally desensitize ourselves in order to survive and move forward. I started thinking about this while dealing with my son's ADHD symptoms years ago. While he was on medication that helped him tremendously during school, it didn't last all day and his hyperactivity and impulsivity would come back in full force once it wore off. He would react inappropriately, both physically and verbally when things didn't go his way, and I felt like I was constantly refereeing things between him and his siblings so that nobody would get hurt.

Years before at my nephew's birthday party, I first realized that I had subconsciously desensitized myself to some of my son's behaviors. Towards the end of the party, one of my relatives snapped at my son and asked him to stop tapping on something in the party room. I think it might have been a fish tank, but what it was doesn't really matter. What matters is that I realized that my son had been tapping on that tank for a long time and it was extremely annoying! But, because it was less annoying or aggressive than other behaviors that he consistently exhibited, I subconsciously tuned it out and I hadn't even noticed he was doing it.

If I had reacted to every one of his annoying hyperactive/impulsive/defiant behaviors every time they happened, I would have spent 24 hours a day yelling at and punishing my son. So, I think I just naturally started tuning some of the less serious things out and didn't even notice them anymore.

I think a similar thing happened with my son's PANS/PANDAS condition, because it became less horrific and more routine for me to reassure my son that I was not an imposter and I was not poisoning his food. I wouldn't have been able to move forward with my everyday life if I broke down in tears whenever he had psychotic thoughts, so my mind subconsciously desensitized itself. This was my own personal defense mechanism, and although I knew that holding my feelings in wasn't healthy, I just had to do it in order to get through the day.

I soon began talking to my own therapist, and it helped to have someone to just listen while I cried my eyes out. I didn't want to put that burden on my friends or family, but it was much easier to lose my shit in front of someone who I was paying to listen.

By the end of January, I started feeling like my son was getting better. He didn't seem to quiz me anymore in order to confirm that I was still his mom, and his calls to me and his dad during the day simmered down. During the previous 3 months, he had to call both me and his dad (whomever he wasn't with in the morning) before he got on the bus to make sure we had our phones with us. He would call us again the second he got off the bus and before he put his phone in the locker to remind us to keep our phones with us throughout the day and to answer our phones when he called. Then, he'd call again as soon as the school bell rang to make sure we were OK. Those extra check in calls also started to simmer down, until they were completely gone.

THE FINANCIAL BURDEN

My son was noticing how much all these appointments and medications were costing us, and I told him not to worry because I had a health insurance account from money that was taken out of my paycheck, and that's what I was using to pay for it. I was only using that to pay for some of the treatments, because I was already taking the max amount allowed out of my paycheck and the money was coming out of that account way faster than my paycheck was putting money back into it.

I didn't want my son to be worried about finances on top of everything else, but it was inevitable, especially with his anxiety at an all time high. He told me I didn't need to buy him any Christmas presents, because he knew he was draining my bank account with all his medical bills. I told him I had plenty of savings (I didn't) and assured him that I wasn't concerned about how much we were spending – I just wanted him to get better and that was the most important thing of all.We were continuing to see a behavioral therapist on a weekly basis, and the out of pocket costs for that were reduced from $150/session to $69/session because my ex-husband's new health insurance covered some of it. That was a relief, because we were still paying 100% out of pocket for our psychiatrist and specialist, both of whom did not take any insurance.

The little savings I had was gone, so I started drawing money out of my retirement funds and drew from my home equity line of credit to keep my finances above water. My ex-husband was contributing to the medical bills, but the cost of care for this was just financially crippling me.

My son was noticing how much all these appointments and medications were costing us, and I told him not to worry because I had a health insurance account from money that was taken out of my paycheck, and that's what I was using to pay for it. I was only using that to pay for some of the treatments, because I was already taking the max amount allowed out of my paycheck and the money was coming out of that account way faster than my paycheck was putting money back into it. I didn't want him to be worried about finances on top of everything else, but of course he did worry.

He told me I didn't need to buy him any Christmas presents, because he knew he was draining my bank account with all his medical bills. I told him I had plenty of savings (I didn't) and assured him that I wasn't concerned about how much we were spending – I just wanted him to get better and that was the most important thing of all.

The cost of care for any mental illness is high, but we also had to add in the cost of seeing the specialist for PANS/PANDAS, and the cost of additional specialists for the various ailments that occupy your son's intrusive thoughts. It's critical to get treatment for this condition early, but insurance doesn't cover most of it because there hasn't been enough research to validate PANS/PANDAS as a real condition with a proven treatment protocol.

In February, I had to trade in my 13year old minivan because it was on its last legs and the engine started leaking. This was literally the worst time for me to add a car payment to my evergrowing list of bills. But, my credit was still good and I needed a reliable car - especially if I was going to continue to drive 2 hours to see the specialist in NJ on a regular basis.

I was reading a post on Facebook by the Foundation for Children with Neuroimmune Disorders, and my heart broke for some of the people who commented on it. The post was a quote from Dr. Frankovich, of Stanford PANS Clinic:

"Prompt treatment may prevent life-long psychiatric illness and other inflammatory sequelae."

Sequelae (which I had to google) refers to a condition which is the consequence of a previous disease or injury.

From Parents of Children with PANS/PANDAS:
"There are few in the medical community curious enough to acknowledge the disorders or wonder at the cause, much less the treatment. And there are less than a few insurance companies that cover the treatment which can be cost prohibitive or can bankrupt a family."

"When they make treatment available for those who aren't well off or have 5 houses to mortgage, more will get help."

"This is all well and good but when you live in a state that refuses to acknowledge that this is a real illness, you're kind of up you know what creek without a paddle."

"Can't afford the treatment for my son. Doctors have gone up against the insurance company but still no luck."

MAKING PROGRESS

In March, it had been 5 months since we started dealing with my son's neuropsychiatric symptoms, thought to be triggered by PANS/PANDAS. I started taking a class offered by the National Alliance for Mental Illness (NAMI) for people who have family members living with mental illness. My son is better, but unfortunately not all better – and I'm trying to learn whatever I can to help him.

I'm still a member of the PANS/PANDAS support groups on Facebook, but I had to stop "following" them. I was seeing too many posts in my newsfeed and I would get consumed with them, reading a vast amount of information and heartbreaking stories about other kids with the same condition. I realized those groups were helping me, but also causing me distress because I was constantly being reminded of the aspects of this horrific condition. I can still click on the groups and read posts or write my own comments, but the posts do not pop up anymore and it's helped me greatly.

We last saw our PANS/PANDAS specialist in Mid-January and we will see him again for a follow up in April. During our last visit, Dr. T said we could start weaning my son off the antibiotics because he seemed to be doing significantly better with his anxiety and paranoia. But although he was no longer questioning whether I was still his mother, he was still having lots of anxiety about his overall health.

He had worries about losing his hearing, having a concussion after a minor collision with a classmate in gym class, internal bleeding because he thought he tasted blood in his mouth, and a fear of contracting salmonella. He hasn't talked to me about the salmonella, but he mentioned this to his psychiatrist in one of his appointments and the psychiatrist shared that with me.

Continuing to search for answers and the right doses of the right medications to help my son, we made some changes to his medications following that appointment in January.

- **Clarithromycin** (Biaxin) Reduced his dose from 500 mg twice a day to 500 mg once a day
- **Valacyclovir** Hydrochloride (Valtrex) - We took the 10-day course of 1g twice a day, prescribed by Dr. T. to address the higher coxsackievirus titers. We finished that in January and are not taking it now.
- **METANYX** (L-methylfolate) once a day – We are continuing to take this.
- **Culturelle Probiotic** (OTC) once a day – We are continuing to take this.
- **Vitamin B-12 Gummies** (OTC) once a day – We stopped taking this per Dr. T's recommendation, because his B-12 levels were better (even higher than the reference range) after his last blood test. He continues to take a daily Flintstones multivitamin.
- **Prozac** – Increased his dose from 10 mg/day to 20 mg/day (went to 15 mg/day for 10 days beginning on 2/20 and began taking 20 mg/day on 3/1/2019)
- **Concerta** – Began a starting dose of 18 mg/day (on school days only) on 1/28/2019 for his ADHD (he was previously on 30 mg of extended release Ritalin – prior to onset of neuropsychiatric symptoms)

I've also read 2 books written about patients who have lived through this and come out on the other (much brighter) side. As I mentioned earlier, I've read *Brain on Fire*, by Susannah Calahan, whose autoimmune encephalitis onset occurred as an adult, and *Saving Sammy*, by Beth Alison Maloney, who is the mother of a boy who had PANDAS as a child.

Both patients are in full remission now, and they inspire me to keep going and keep asking questions until I can save my own son from this horrible disorder. Until then, I remind myself of a quote I read from David Sheff, who was recovering from his son's addiction: "I didn't cause it. I can't control it. I can't cure it."

Although, PANS/PANDAS is not addiction, I have to remind myself that no matter how much research I do, I won't be able to control this disorder and I won't be able to cure it. At the onset of my son's symptoms, I couldn't stop reading about PANS/PANDAS. I was determined to figure out how to "cure" my son.

One of the parents in a PANS/PANDAS support group on Facebook told me that treatment for this disorder is like a marathon, and she was 100% right. I wanted to sprint to my son's recovery, but I had to learn that it was a slow process of learning what was going on inside his body and carefully working with doctors to find the right mix of medicine for his unique body.

Right now, there isn't one magical treatment to "cure" PANS/PANDAS, and every patient responds differently to the various treatments that have been shown to improve symptoms in different patients.

Fortunately, we've been able to improve my son's condition with the help of some very smart, forward-thinking doctors who aren't afraid to think out of the box and treat this condition. There isn't enough research to validate the various treatments available for these patients, so many doctors do not treat it, and some have not even heard about it.

As a result, there are many children who suffer for years without treatment or with the wrong treatment, and many of them are in and out of mental hospitals, because there isn't enough known about how to treat PANS/PANDAS.

Abraham Lincoln once wrote, "I am now the most miserable man living. If what I feel were equally distributed to the whole human family, there would not be one cheerful face on the earth. Whether I shall ever be better I can not tell; I awfully forebode I shall not. To remain as I am is impossible; I must die or be better, it appears to me."

Although we have come a long way in mental health treatment since Abraham Lincoln's time, we have a very long way to go. People are suffering from PANS/PANDAS and other mental illnesses, and access to treatment is difficult, even for those who are willing to pay outside of what their insurance covers.

As I continue to stand by my son's side as he recovers from this illness, I am grateful for many of the blessings we have, even amidst the chaos we've experienced over the past 5 months. My son's recovery has been slow with baby steps each day, and sometimes it's difficult to notice his improvement. But, when I look back to where we were on that awful day in September - and for several weeks after that - I can see that he is better. He's not "all better," but he's better.

Although finding a psychiatrist for my son was way more difficult than I could have ever anticipated, the person who we found is one of the many angels who has helped us throughout this journey. He is one of the small percentage of healthcare professionals who is aware of PANDAS and knew to test for strep antibodies.

My son is healing because this doctor knew about a very rare condition and was able to lead us down the right path. We are still tweaking meds, but we're moving in the right direction.

The behavioral therapist who agreed to meet with us on the second day of my son's psychosis continues to meet with him every week, and she has been instrumental in providing him with strategies to question his intrusive thoughts and work through his anxiety.

Our PANS/PANDAS specialist has been another key player in

my son's treatment. The tests he ran told us so much about the root causes of my son's condition, and I am grateful that we have the means to be able to work with him.

I know we still have a long way to go on my son's treatment journey. But, we're moving in the right direction, and I am thankful for that.

Weight Loss

Intermittent fasting can be a simple and effective way to lose weight when done properly, as regular short-term fasts can help you consume fewer calories and shed pounds.

A number of studies suggest that intermittent fasting is as effective as traditional calorie-restricted diets for short-term weight loss .

A 2018 review of studies in overweight adults found intermittent fasting led to an average weight loss of 15 lbs (6.8 kg) over the course of 3–12 months.

Another review showed intermittent fasting reduced body weight by 3–8% in overweight or obese adults over a period of 3–24 weeks. The review also found that participants reduced their waist circumference by 3–7% over the same period .

It should be noted that the long-term effects of intermittent fasting on weight loss for women remain to be seen.

In the short term, intermittent fasting seems to aid in weight loss. However, the amount you lose will likely depend on the number of calories you consume during non-fasting periods and how long you adhere to the lifestyle.

It May Help You Eat Less

Switching to intermittent fasting may naturally help you eat less.

One study found that young men ate 650 fewer calories per day when their food intake was restricted to a four-hour window .

Another study in 24 healthy men and women looked at the effects of a long, 36-hour fast on eating habits. Despite consuming extra calories on the post-fast day, participants dropped their total calorie balance by 1,900 calories, a significant reduction .

Other Health Benefits

A number of human and animal studies suggest that intermittent fasting may also yield other health benefits.

Reduced inflammation: Some studies show that intermittent fasting can reduce key markers of inflammation.

RESOURCES

One of the most helpful websites I found throughout my research is nepans.org. It's run the the New England PANS/PANDAS Network, and it contains handouts that explain the condition in simple terms. I used some of their pdfs for a meeting at my son's school, and it was helpful to have information from a third party to refer to as we worked to update my son's IEP to accomodate his illness.

It's also important to know that you're not alone. Seek information in whatever way works best for you, because this is a difficult journey and knowing that you're not alone is very helpful. Read stories that give you hope, because sometimes that's all you will have to hang onto when you are feeling helpless and hopeless.

And most importantly, take care of yourself. Tending to your sleep, nutrition and overall well being will give you the strength you need to care for your child.

www.ingramcontent.com/pod-product-compliance
Lightning Source LLC
Chambersburg PA
CBHW072027280526
45788CB00007B/2700